I0830288

WHERE DID THE **UNITED STATES** OF **AMERICA** GO?

DOUGLAS WASHINGTON

authorHOUSE

AuthorHouse™
1663 Liberty Drive
Bloomington, IN 47403
www.authorhouse.com
Phone: 1 (800) 839-8640

© 2019 Douglas Washington. All rights reserved.

No part of this book may be reproduced, stored in a retrieval system, or transmitted by any means without the written permission of the author.

Published by AuthorHouse 10/11/2019

ISBN: 978-1-7283-3159-1 (sc)
ISBN: 978-1-7283-3158-4 (e)

Print information available on the last page.

Any people depicted in stock imagery provided by Getty Images are models, and such images are being used for illustrative purposes only.
Certain stock imagery © Getty Images.

This book is printed on acid-free paper.

Because of the dynamic nature of the Internet, any web addresses or links contained in this book may have changed since publication and may no longer be valid. The views expressed in this work are solely those of the author and do not necessarily reflect the views of the publisher, and the publisher hereby disclaims any responsibility for them.

AUTHOR'S NOTE

I WROTE THIS MANUSCRIPT under the pen name of Douglas Washington. These two names represent the middle names of my father and his twin brother—two men I loved, respected, and admired.

CONTENTS

Preface ix

Consensus, Compromise, Greed, and Selfishness 1
Who Are We Really as a Nation? 3
What Is Happening to Our Governing Strategy? 5
Who Is Causing the Severe Changes? 7
Representation and Majority Rules? 11
Communication: Nonfiction, Fiction, and Fake News .. 13
Communication: Respectful, Secure Winners or
    Disrespectful, Insecure Losers 15
Do We Respect Freedom of Speech? 19
Freedom for Religion and Freedom from Religion 21
Abortion: What Is the Real Issue? 23
The Integrity of the Constitution and the Supreme
    Court 25
Who Determines the Role and Size of Government? 29
Healthcare and the Free Market System 31
Immigration: Who Are We and Who Do We Want
    to Be? 35
Gun Rights or Gun Control: To Have Guns or to
    Not Have Guns—Is That the Question? 39

Yes, the Climate Is Changing! 41

Where Do We Want the United States of America
to Go? 45

Conclusion 49

About the Author 53

About the Book 55

PREFACE

Our national values and governing structures, as well as our way of life, are under attack today from within and from outside our nation. Internally we are destroying the state of our union, and some of us do not recognize that it is happening. Dictator nations, socialist nations, religious nations, and communist nations are becoming more and more successful undermining the state of our union, and they are enjoying and celebrating the severe divisiveness that has been created among American citizens.

I have children and grandchildren. The state of our union and where our union is going are personal and emotional to me. My motivation behind writing this manuscript was to articulate what I believe is the current state of our union. The purpose was to help me better understand and cope with the changes that are influencing the state of our union and to determine what my suggestions would be to improve it. I come from a background of "Don't put a complaint or a problem in the suggestion box unless you have a suggestion to correct the complaint or solve the problem."

There are two statements that are guiding principles behind the approach and method used to write this manuscript. One is "I don't think I can make this complicated enough for you to understand." I have been accused of overly evaluating circumstances and situations. I have chosen not to do that in this manuscript. The second statement is "There are liars, damn liars, and statisticians." We all know that you can make statistics say just about anything you want them to say. (I reference you to "political polls.") I have chosen not to use statistical tools in this manuscript. I have a couple of exceptions that you will notice. Nobody's perfect.

I was watching a documentary several years ago concerning the Civil War. A southern historian made the statement that a "true democracy" is built on compromise and that the United States of America had been built on compromise but in 1860 failed to compromise.

Decision-making is difficult when an individual has two extremes to choose from. First, you only have two choices, and second, when you make your choice, it is usually either a win/lose or lose/lose decision. When this environment of extreme choices exists with a group of two or more people (e.g., business group, local government, state government, and national government) the decision-making process becomes more difficult. When there are extreme emotions and/or short time restraints, decision-making becomes even more difficult. When the outcome has the potential to impact a situation, such as a possible national emergency, decision-making becomes much more difficult.

If there is not an individual thought process or a group decision-making process that includes compromise and consensus building, the outcome will be gridlock because greed and selfishness already dominate the process.

CONSENSUS, COMPROMISE, GREED, AND SELFISHNESS

It is important to start by explaining consensus, compromise, greed, and selfishness as they relate to the environments I will be writing about; our nation, our governing structures and processes, and some of the current divisive issues. I will also include some ideas concerning what I believe is contributing to the divisiveness that has created some of the problems we have with these issues.

All four—consensus, compromise, greed, and selfishness—can be good and positive, and all four can be bad and negative. Consensus and compromise do not mean that there is no room for emotional expression, discussion, or negotiation. The right of expression is the fabric of our nation, as stated in the First Amendment. An element of greed and selfishness is involved in the emotion of defending your desires and rights. Consensus and compromise do not mean giving up or giving in to someone else's desires or rights, nor do greed and selfishness mean being so self-centered that you do not understand or care about another person's desires and rights. Consensus and compromise do not imply agreeing only when you think they are the best option; they also require agreement even though you might think that a better option may exist. Greed and selfishness do not mean that you can't understand and accept someone's values and beliefs that are different from yours. Consensus and compromise do not mean the outcome will be a moderate decision. Greed and selfishness do not mean the outcome will not be a moderate decision. Consensus and compromise can be giving and taking. They can be giving in order to take. Greed and selfishness can be giving and taking. They can be taking in order to give.

The goal would be to balance all four: consensus, compromise, greed, and selfishness. Being in balance does not mean all four are equal. Do not view balance as 25 percent consensus, 25 percent compromise, 25 percent greed, and 25 percent selfishness. The challenge of balance exists in the environment, the degree, and the impact of the outcome. You can go out of balance and still be successful, but if one or more of the four dominates the environment, the degree, or the outcome, you will most likely not be successful.

Do not view this as conservative versus liberal versus independent. It is probably naïve to think you can keep politics out of a discussion; however, the goal is to let the process of decision-making determine the focus, direction, content, and outcome.

WHO ARE WE REALLY AS A NATION?

Our Founding Fathers put in place what I believe is the best structure for creating an environment to govern. The structures that exist for making decisions in any local, state, or federal government in the United States are sound and proven. The foundations that these structures exist on are freedom of democracy, freedom of individual rights, and freedom of the market economy. The three branches of government are not only structured for a checks-and-balances approach but for gathering a cross section of diverse representation. Properly utilized, this organizational structure can gather individuals who can bring the diverse knowledge and experience necessary to represent all people from their elected part of our nation.

The problem is not the structure but the gerrymandering of the structure and the politics of the process. When we try to manipulate the structure so that one specific ideology is the dominant majority, in one or all, of the three branches of government, the structure loses credibility and effectiveness. When we continually change the political governing rules to benefit one ideology, we lose stability in the three branches of government. When we manipulate the voting structure of voting districts to the advantage of one political ideology at the expense of another political ideology for the purpose of having a majority, or when we manipulate voting processes to the extent that voters do not have access to their voting rights, we not only lose credibility, effectiveness, and stability in the political process but are undermining the foundation of our democracy. Add the motivation of needing to be reelected to the lack of credibility, effectiveness, and stability and you have the additional potential of losing the trust in and integrity of not just the structure and process for making decisions but the trust in and integrity of our three branches of government. These components can adversely affect the ability to compromise or reach consensus. If there are not processes and procedures to help clarify decision-making, we usually see greed and selfishness—on rare occasions this can be consensus and compromise—dominating the process.

Somewhere in the structure there needs to be someone or some group as free from political influence as possible to independently help the structure effectively discuss issues for the purpose of reaching a balance between consensus, compromise, greed, and selfishness. No process or structure is completely free of politics. We must allow our system of governing to function the way it was intended to function. If we don't, our best system of governing will become dysfunctional and negatively marginalized from within. We must protect our special environment and structure for governing "of the people, by the people, and for the people."

WHAT IS HAPPENING TO OUR GOVERNING STRATEGY?

My uncle saw a commentary on a news channel a few years ago that stated, "In less than one hundred years, the United States of America will not exist." As he and I discussed this, our first question was whether, or not, this was a joke. My uncle said, "Where do they think the United States of America is going to go?" How could something that sounds so ridiculous happen? We must protect our government and the people it serves. Our country today is divided to an extent that I have not witnessed in my lifetime. I was born in the forties. I am afraid that when people say that their commitment is to God, family, and country, what they are really saying is God, family, and political ideology.

I saw a metaphor about commitment in a movie a few years ago. The actor used the example of walking down a road. Walking down the left side of the road is okay and less dangerous and walking down the right side of the road is okay and less dangerous but walking down the middle of the road is not okay and extremely dangerous.

The current political situation and political party system

in our country can be described the same way. Democrats believe being on the left side is safe and less dangerous for our country, and Republicans believe being on the right side is safe and less dangerous. It seems that both the left and the right view being moderate as being less safe and more dangerous. (Note that I define moderates as moderate Democrats and moderate Republicans. The category of independents in today's politics can be far left, far right, or moderate.)

I can further use my imaginary road to describe our governing strategy. Our governing strategy is to drive down the right lane of this four-lane highway for four to eight years, then to drive down the left lane of this four-lane highway for four to eight years, then to change back to the right, and so on. At times, our operating strategies look like a driver under the influence. Changing lanes is not the reason we look like a drunk driver. Our nation looks out of control because the lane changing is so severe, we are running off the highway on both sides and causing gridlock and tragedies. We must correct this before we cause a national vehicular homicide.

Who is driving this political vehicle?

WHO IS CAUSING THE SEVERE CHANGES?

Most Americans today believe that our country is in a difficult state. We lack faith in the government and our elected officials. I recently read that Americans' confidence in Congress had reached the lowest level ever: 18 percent. That is an astoundingly low level. The people in the United States do not believe Congress has the capacity to make the right decisions nor to operate the government to the voting public's satisfaction. We are having more and more gridlock situations and recently had the longest government shutdown in history.

Many American citizens say that it is the fault of the elected officials and that they should be replaced. Many of these citizens recommend that we replace all the officials but the ones they voted for. Others recommend we only get rid of those officials who do not have the same political views as their own. People from countries that have more than two political parties say that the more political parties they have, the less chance they have of getting what they want. In other words, the focus is not on what is best for the country but what is best for the individual. When consensus and compromise are not part of the decision-making process, greed and selfishness will become the dominant focus of the process.

Two of the three branches of government are made up of the individuals that the people of the United States elected to represent them. These individuals were elected because they promised to go to Washington and vote a certain way, usually to get those who voted for them what they want. It is my belief that those elected officials are doing exactly what they were elected to do. The extreme divide in the representation in the United States government mirrors the extreme divide that exists in the people of our nation. The problems and gridlock are not just reflected in the representation in Washington but primarily in the voting citizens of the United States. If a representative does not satisfy their constituency, he or she will not be reelected. Therefore, we have elected a government that cannot function without gridlock, because we elected a government to make no compromises or reach any consensus.

The people of the United States are to blame for the actions or inactions of the government because of our expectations of what we want our elected officials to do—and our adversaries, around the world and in our country, are absolutely celebrating and excited about it. I remind you of the old saying "I want everyone in government removed except the ones I voted for." I don't believe too many people, if any, could get elected on a platform of "I am going to Washington to compromise and reach a consensus."

Congress has a procedure for negotiating gridlock. A committee of Congressional representatives from each party (Democratic, Republican, and independents) is convened to develop a "compromised plan." My concern with this process and structure is that the primary motivation driving the discussion will be the next election rather than what is best concerning the gridlock issue. The best group to reach a consensus and compromise will be stakeholders who are more concerned with the issue of gridlock than the issue of reelection. This could be a group of elected representatives and stakeholders but coordinated independently. *Independently* means by someone who is not a politician or stakeholder. We must protect our form of government, which was originally designed to include consensus and compromise as cornerstones to our nation's success.

REPRESENTATION AND MAJORITY RULES?

IN A COMMERCIAL I recently saw, a veteran stated that he served so that the majority could rule. With all due respect to that veteran, our military is there for all people in the United States of America. Only a person who voted for the incumbents in office would think that they only served for the majority.

Most elections in the United States, whether local, state, or national, are decided by approximately 5 percent. That means that the winners are elected by approximately 50 (plus or minus 5) percent of the people voting. The politician in the elected official will claim, "The people have spoken, and we will do what they elected us to do." Although 45 (plus or minus 5) percent of the people who voted wanted something else, the elected official will probably only represent 50 (plus or minus 5) percent of their local, state, or national population. Add the electoral college to the mix and you have an even more confused comparison for politicians to use to defend their positions concerning majority rule. I doubt that any politician will tell you they are only representing 50 percent of their voting public. I suggest you look at voting records and policy changes for the facts on who they are representing. I am not questioning the voting process or the electoral college to determine who represents us. I am questioning the reasoning that 50 percent means you represent only those who voted for you. That approach to representation is almost a guarantee of failure in most organizations, including our country.

I often have heard people say, "What we need is someone with a business background to be our representative, governor, or president." If that person were to run the government the way they run their business, they might be successful but would probably not be reelected. Most successful businesses are run with the entire organizational needs as part of the focus of decision-making. They cannot shut down parts of their business because of gridlock decision-making and expect to be successful. If our elected officials do not represent with compromise and consensus as part of their actions (not words), their actions as representatives will be dominated by greed and selfishness.

COMMUNICATION: NONFICTION, FICTION, AND FAKE NEWS

I HEARD A FICTIONAL story about a person whose words went out of their mouth and into their ears and they thought that two people had just agreed with them. It made them feel so good that they continued talking. The more they talked, the more they believed that more people were agreeing with them. Soon the only words that the person would listen to were words that sounded like the words coming out of their mouth. They would hear other words, but rather than listening to other words, they would be thinking of the words coming out of their own mouth. They also believed that if they interrupted the conversation by continuing to say the same words over and over, the people they were talking to would listen to them. The problem was the people they were talking to were only hearing and not listening because they, too, were thinking of their own words to say over and over by interrupting and responding. There is a saying for this type of communications. "Those who think they know it all frustrate those of us who do know it all." This maybe fictional, but does it sound familiar?

We have many forms of communications today. We have an enormous selection of cable, television, radio, and social media options as sources of the information we receive. Many people make their decisions on which form of communication to use based on the same principals as the people who like to hear themselves talk. They will not watch, listen to, or read words that do not sound like the words that are coming out of their mouths. They will tell you to be careful of certain news programs and the social media because not everything you hear or read is true; however, their interpretations of "true" or "not true" is based on the words coming out of their mouths. What they watch, listen to, or read, which is based on the words coming out of their mouths, is true, and everything else is not true. A favorite expression for words that do not sound like the words coming out of their mouths is "fake news."

There is a tremendous amount of information available to people through the technologies of social media, television, radio, the internet, etc. The good news is all these forms of communication have become very effective at giving information based on the words coming out of your mouth. The bad news is all these forms of communication have become very effective at giving information based on the words coming out of your mouth. The main reason they are so effective is they are usually the sources that originally gave you the words that are coming out of your mouth. While in a nonfictional sense this maybe a form of brainwashing, I do not believe this is the real problem in balancing consensus, compromise, greed, and selfishness in communications.

COMMUNICATION: RESPECTFUL, SECURE WINNERS OR DISRESPECTFUL, INSECURE LOSERS

THE MOST CONCERNING PROBLEM we have today is not talking. If someone can talk you into something, someone else can talk you out of it. The most concerning problem we have is the respect of listening. If we cannot allow ourselves to listen to, not just hear, information coming from people with different values and beliefs, we will become partially illiterate to what is going on around us and incapable of understanding or accepting compromise or consensus. We must learn to listen to words and beliefs we disagree with. We must try to understand why someone believes differently from how we believe. We have become a very divisive country. Our country depends on the voting public to be literate. I am not talking about changing people's beliefs. I am talking about respecting people's beliefs. If we do not become literate, greed and selfishness will become our primary communication motivation.

I am not trying to belittle or degrade media in the United

States. There are many different media organizations, with varying motivations, and they are all specialized to their identified target groups. I believe most of our choices are professional and highly talented. Our challenges, as readers, viewers, and listeners, is to remember to make the distinction between journalist and entertainer. I recently read a new word for me. The word is *politainment.* (It is so new that my spell-check doesn't recognize it.) The word represents the growing field of political entertainment. We must be able to distinguish between fictional political entertainment and nonfictional journalistic reporting. This can be very challenging at times.

We participate with entertainment. We choose the movies/programs we want to watch, the music we want to listen to, and the books/magazines we want to read. If we don't like what we are reading, seeing, or listening to, we throw it away, turn it off, or tune it out. Journalism is to give us facts concerning issues. It is not something we usually participate with. We are usually focused on learning and gathering information to become more literate. That is another reason why I believe if we are not getting our information from a variety of different sources, including those outside our ideology, we will become illiterate to what are truly the issues and facts available to us. You can be your own judge. Are you seeking entertainment to read, watch, or listen to the words you like, or are you seeking information to be literate concerning the issues? Another way to judge yourself is when you are reading about, watching, or listening to someone you do not agree with, the words coming out of someone else's mouth, are your thoughts focused on trying to understand why that individual believes what they are saying? Or are you thinking about what your rebuttal, the words coming out of your mouth, is.

The second most concerning communication problem is about talking. The words coming out of our mouths are becoming more and more divisive. Someone I respect was teaching me about "winners" and "losers." He told me that one way I could know who the true "loser" is would be when they are insecure and believe they cannot meet the standard of a "winner," the "loser" will do whatever it takes to bring the "winner" down to their level. This could be by bending or breaking the rules or manipulating the situation to their advantage. In most situations, the "loser" will use negative comments. The lesson was when you lose, do not become a "loser." Respect the "winner," and do your best to improve.

This was a very difficult lesson as a young man and at times has been a difficult lesson to follow throughout my life. I can tell you through personal experiences that there are many people who have trouble with this lesson. This "loser" mentality has become standard rebuttal in debates and discussions in our society. The text of the programming we read, watch, and listen to has developed a negative-attack mentality for the readers, listeners, and viewers to absorb. Does "deflect and attack" sound familiar? We see this in political and nonpolitical programming and discussions. When a politician believes they are in a negative position ("losing") in the polls, journalistic reports, or political entertainment, they will turn to negative attack responses focused on the opposing person/ideology or journalistic source of the information or political entertainer. The most disturbing part of this situation for me is when the "loser" attacks negatively, bends or breaks the rules, or manipulates the situation, usually their approval rating among their ideology followers (Democrat, Republican, independent) goes up. This behavior rewards "loser" mentality. The effect is to showcase the "ideology" (Democrat, Republican, independent) as insecure losers to our nation and to the world. Those who are members of the ideology on the attack believe they are "winners." This is another example of winning the battle but losing the war.

We have become a nation of disrespectful, insecure "losers" when it comes to our communications and actions. I have already stated that freedom is our foundation, and the fabric of our nation is freedom of expression. The word *fabric* denotes the extreme and numerous diversity we have in America. We must find a way to positively unite all these wonderful ideas and beliefs into our country's communication styles, structures, and processes. We need to become respectful, secure "Winners."

DO WE RESPECT FREEDOM OF SPEECH?

THERE IS A FRENCH saying that, when translated into English, states, "I may not agree with what you are saying, but I will give my life for you to have the freedom to say it." We, as Americans, state over and over that we will fight and die for our freedoms, which includes freedom of speech. Do we, or do we only when the words are words we want to listen to? We will always have someone or some group who will stretch the truth and find a way to challenge our beliefs or values. We are experiencing that today with social media, demonstrations, speeches, group meetings, political rhetoric, etc. We are having one of our foundational beliefs and values challenged today. How we handle it will determine whether we are serious about freedom of speech.

Emotionally charged demonstrations, counterdemonstrations, marches, town hall meetings, political rhetoric, etc. are not new. We experienced similar events during the civil rights movement and the Vietnam War demonstrations in the 1950s, 1960s, and 1970s. As a nation, we stood up against those who would try to stop legal freedom of speech. It has become a priority to stand up again. Some of our national leaders and many Americans have taken freedom of speech and defined it as "If I agree with what you are saying, you are free to talk. If I do not agree with what you are saying, I will try to stop you from talking." Demonstrations, counterdemonstrations, marches, town hall meetings, political rhetoric, etc. are core freedom of speech vehicles. Unfortunately, we have successful businesses in our country whose services are to provide training on how to disrupt these core vehicles of freedom of speech.

The social media and internet vehicle have changed what many Americans consider "free speech." This communication vehicle will redefine the definition of safe and legal free speech. We need to be very careful with the process to redefine freedom of speech. Hopefully, it will be a process that will balance consensus, compromise, greed, and selfishness and not be determined by political ideology. The definition of *freedom of speech* has become so blurred by political ideology that we are divided on the true definition. More importantly, we are divided on the true importance of the value of freedom of speech. I hope we are not losing our respect for the right to free speech.

FREEDOM FOR RELIGION AND FREEDOM FROM RELIGION

I RECENTLY SAW A political cartoon that showed two Native Americans on a hilltop in twenty-first-century America overlooking the ocean. A sixteenth- or seventeenth-century boat was sailing off into the sunset. The caption read, "They are leaving to find a place where they can find freedom of religion." We have today a very divisive and emotional discussion about the separation of church and state. Making that decision in today's environment of extreme beliefs will be extremely detrimental to religious groups and their freedom for religion and to those who currently feel discriminated against and are seeking freedom from religion. The politics of religion has become so extreme with emotionally charged divisive disagreements that it has become difficult to distinguish what is politics and what is religion. The line between politics and religion has become so blurred that it is hard to see an ending that would be either win/win or win/lose. We are demeaning religion in America through political involvement and rhetoric. The course we are on is lose/lose.

Our origin as a country was not intended to be a blur between government and religion or a "church state." It was an origin of balance between religion and government or "freedom of religion." Religion can be one of the most divisive issues a nation can face. World and American history include many tragic examples of what can happen if we do not find a balance between government and religion.

Religion does and will always have an influence on our United States of America, and it should. However, there are religious organizations in our country that are involved in politics to the point that it appears their goal is to have a church state under their religious sect's beliefs. Members of these religious sects have already begun dividing the country on religious and political issues. If we want to have true freedom of religion in this country, we are going to need to add compromise and consensus to the discussions and rhetoric because greed and selfishness are only creating divisiveness and gridlock on this issue in our country.

ABORTION: WHAT IS THE REAL ISSUE?

THE ISSUE OF ABORTION is severely dividing our nation. We will not be able to resolve this issue in our courts, in our churches, or in our government separately. Before *Roe versus Wade,* we had a severe divide in our country, and we have a severe divide today. We are also in a lose/lose situation with the abortion issue. This is only one of the issues that will not be decided by the political ideology in power. To use an old expression again, "You may be winning the battle, but you are losing the war."

We seem to treat the abortion issue as if demonstrations, politicians, or the US Supreme Court will hold the final decision. This will not be the case. It has not been the answer in the past, nor will it be in the future. There also appears to be no middle ground (consensus or compromise) available.

One side of the issue believes if abortion was illegal it would stop or reduce abortions. Before *Roe versus Wade,* it did neither. Our nation's history, whether good or bad, tells us that making something illegal does not always work out the way we hoped for. Prohibition, for all the right reasons, was not the law needed to solve the real issue.

The other side of the abortion issue believes a woman should have the right to make the decisions concerning her body. While this may be true, a decision to have an abortion stops a life. This decision should not be taken lightly, and for many women, this decision is probably the most difficult decision that they will make in their lives. However, we are a better country than to have a medical procedure that stops a life and not take some action to better manage and utilize this procedure.

Passing a law to make abortions legal or illegal will not solve the abortion issue, so why would you celebrate the passage or court ruling? What would you be celebrating? I don't know unless both sides have reached a point where they are focused on legality or their self, religious, or political conscience rather than solving the issue of abortion. I do know that among the legal, healthcare, social services, education, and religious communities we have the people who can jointly develop the best recommendations concerning how we deal with abortion, if they are not impeded by greed and selfishness.

THE INTEGRITY OF THE CONSTITUTION AND THE SUPREME COURT

Some will say that we have the document that we need to help us resolve conflict in the United States, and that document is the Constitution. I agree that this document serves that purpose and is the foundation for effective conflict resolution and decision-making. The ultimate interpretation of this document comes from the US Supreme Court. Nine very knowledgeable and dedicated individuals. As much as they would like to be known as being independent of politics, they are not. Recent political actions associated with the selection of Supreme Court justices have negatively affected its credibility. The justices will do their best to judge independently, but their credibility has been tarnished by political gerrymandering of the selection process and structure. I am also reading that consideration is being given to increasing the number of justices. The motivation is political ideology. This would further negatively affect the credibility of the Supreme Court and our governing structure.

There are two very special documents in my life: the US Constitution and the Bible. Both were written and revised by inspired men and women. The information and ideas in both documents help me resolve conflicts and make decisions. Both documents, however, are open to individual interpretation. When I hear someone say, "We need someone in this position who knows the Constitution [or knows the Bible]," I become skeptical. I'm afraid what they are saying is "We need someone whose interpretation of the Constitution [or Bible] is the same as mine." The documents were written over two hundred and two thousand years ago respectively. They have been interpreted many times by many different people. As stated, they are "living, breathing" documents that have stood the test of time. However, we view these documents today through a twenty-first-century lens. Both documents have been affected by politics over the years and still survive as documents we can discuss and depend on. We have constitutional judges and biblical scholars to help us with that task, but implementation becomes almost an individual decision. The success of these two documents is only limited by the individuals and timely interpretations of those reading them.

Please understand that I view the Constitution as the primary document for government-related legal conflict resolution and decision-making. The Bible is the primary document for individual conflict resolution and decision-making relative to how I should live my life. We must protect the distinctiveness of each of these two documents. The unique purpose of each of these two documents should remain separate, or we could create the same problem we have with freedom of religion. We do not want to demean either of these two documents.

Other religions have their equivalent document to the Bible that should be respected as well.

27

WHO DETERMINES THE ROLE AND SIZE OF GOVERNMENT?

Two of the most pressing questions today are "What is the role of government?" and "Why is the government as large as it is?" There are probably more opinions and answers to these two questions than there are opinions and answers to the questions concerning any other issue. That being the case, I will add one more opinion to the mix.

History has taught us that whatever we as individuals, groups, businesses and organizations (for-profit or nonprofit), religions, cities, towns, states, nation, etc. cannot handle, without negatively affecting our national stability, the government will handle. If "We the People" do not properly resolve the issues and problems we have as a nation, the government will step in to resolve the issues and problems. Another way of looking at this is that "We the People" have had numerous opportunities to resolve the problems and issues, and because of a lack of balancing compromise, consensus, greed, and selfishness, we created divisiveness and gridlock. Examples can be found under the categories of civil rights, religious rights, labor laws, business laws, health laws, educational laws, etc.

For those of us who would like to see a smaller government, here is our opportunity. We are the reason that our government is so large. We have not been able to solve problems and issues, but we blame the government for being large because we have not been willing to accept the responsibility for the problems that exist. We are a democracy. We should get the first opportunity to correct the issue or solve our own problems. That is what a true democracy does. It is time for us to start acting like a true democracy. Put the nation's future back in the hands of the American people. This will not be accomplished with an imbalance of greed and selfishness. Greed and selfishness have made our government larger, not smaller.

HEALTHCARE AND THE FREE MARKET SYSTEM

A PRIME EXAMPLE OF the role and size of government is our current healthcare system and the relationship to our free market economic system. We probably have the best healthcare of any nation. Many people will come from all over the world to get what they believe is the best healthcare in the world. Our healthcare system, however, has been in a state of flux for many years. It was an issue when I began my voting career in the late '60s, but civil rights and the Vietnam War were the dominate issues then.

Healthcare availability and cost became an even more critical issue in the '90s. Since 1992 we have had a Democratic president for eight years, a Republican president for eight years, another Democratic president for eight years, and currently another Republican president. During the terms of these four presidents, the Senate and House of Representatives have changed political ideology leadership several times. Healthcare, including prescription costs, has escalated during all the presidential terms since 1992. Availability had increased, but political efforts are trying to reduce that availability to some Americans. The reason for the reduction is the belief that most Americans would prefer lower costs and more choices rather than availability. The research, depending on which political ideology information you chose, will both defend and reject that position. (Liars, damn liars, and statisticians.)

Since 1992, two healthcare systems have been developed. One healthcare system, "The Patient Protection and Affordable Care Act," is a United States federal statute enacted by the 111th United States Congress and signed into law in 2010. The statute was passed and signed into law during a time when one political ideology controlled the Congress and the White House. Since implementation, Congress and the White House, both of a different political ideology than the one when signed into law, have actively tried to remove the healthcare system as an option. No other healthcare system has been presented to the American people as an option. Many individual and specifically targeted options have been made available, both to help or dismantle the current system. None has successfully reduced cost, increased availability, or provided coordination and stability to our healthcare system as a whole system.

Congress and the White House have spent a great deal of time talking about what is wrong with our healthcare system but very little time talking about what to do about it. As a result, the American people have grown very frustrated and are divided along political ideologies. I wish the same effort to remove or maintain the current healthcare system had been applied with the balance of consensus and compromise rather than the dominate imbalance of greed and selfishness. What we currently have is a healthcare environment that is sporadic and in noncoordinating pieces.

A healthcare system currently under consideration would operate similarly to our Medicare healthcare system. This effort is being developed by the political ideology that developed the 2010 statute with no input from the other ideology that wants to remove the 2010 statute. Whether this system will reduce or stabilize cost and increase availability, I do not know. Whether this system will have adequate choices, I do not know. Whether this system will provide the quality of healthcare the American people deserve, I do not know. Whether this system will help stabilize the coordination of healthcare services, I do not know. Whether our healthcare stakeholders have been involved, I do not know. What I do know is that this will be government run and coordinated and not run or coordinated by our free market system. Government would be stepping in to resolve what our free market and political systems have failed to do.

Some have used the rational (excuse) that one healthcare system cannot serve all Americans. There is usually more than one system working collaboratively with each other in larger and more complicated structures. Being large and complicated has not stopped the American people before when they truly wanted something as important as healthcare. I find it very hard to believe that we do not have the resources of people with the knowledge and motivation to develop a healthcare system. We have many knowledgeable, qualified, and motivated individuals associated with the healthcare markets and the healthcare profession that deliver the products and services to the American people. Rather than continuing to develop noncoordinating healthcare-related pieces, developing a government-coordinated healthcare system, or continuing the political ideology arguments and efforts to revise or dismantle the current statute, why don't we develop a process to study and develop a healthcare system that is influenced by both our healthcare professionals and our free market systems with help from government related sources?

If a market-driven healthcare system that provides the American people with the coordination, stability, quality, cost, choice, and availability they deserve cannot be developed and implemented because of greed and selfishness in our free market and political environment, our government will be forced to develop a system because "We the People," our free market economic system, and our political structure created gridlock rather than solving the problem. "We the People" are better than this. If America has the best healthcare in the world, then Americans deserve the best healthcare system. Communication, distorted by political ideology, has created so many factually untrue statements that the American people are divided into political camps and no one is asking the real questions that need to be asked before any healthcare system can function properly.

IMMIGRATION: WHO ARE WE AND WHO DO WE WANT TO BE?

IMMIGRATION IS SUFFERING FROM the same national crisis as healthcare. Communication, distorted by political ideology, has created so many factually untrue statements the American people are divided into political camps and no one is asking the real questions that need to be asked before immigration can function properly. The people who are probably the most frustrated are those dedicated homeland security and immigration government employees who are charged with doing their jobs in an environment of "political ping-pong."

Immigration issues are not going to be resolved until someone takes a leadership role that is not primarily politically motivated. Fair and secure immigration is not just driven by security measures. We have become so consumed by the political rhetoric that we have lost sight of the values that have built and should govern this great nation. We have reached a point where authoritative dictatorial leadership is considering undermining the US Constitution and political denial has become rampant.

It is not uncommon for individuals and groups in the United States to create the preconceived solution syndrome when making decisions. This happens more during campaigns, but politicians are not the only ones responsible for this syndrome. I have seen it in my nonpolitical career experiences, and many of our "political entertainment" programs are driven by it. Preconceived solution syndrome occurs when someone determines what they consider to be the solution to an issue or problem. At that point, the individual or group will begin gathering information and discussing that solution. A great deal of time, money and energy may go into substantiating that solution. Once this commitment (time, money, and energy) has been made, there becomes a "no turning back" attitude and commitment to that solution. On some rare occasions, individuals and groups, to justify the time, money, and energy, have created the problem after the solution was developed.

The potential mistakes with preconceived solution syndrome are that it may not be the best solution to the problem, or it may not even be the problem. (I reference you to our current problems and issues concerning abortion, healthcare, immigration, and gun rights). An old saying, we all know is "You can't see the forest for the trees." We are wasting a great deal of time, energy, and money arguing about trees and not looking at what affect the trees have on the forest, and we are not focused on the real problems in the forest. We need decision-making processes that start by discussing and studying the issues and problems and do not start by discussing potential solutions.

We have a history of reacting negatively and slowly to immigration changes in our nation. Just ask the Native

Americans (oh wait—we were the immigrants in that case), the African Americans (oh wait—we paid to bring them to the United States and took their freedom away), the Japanese Americans (oh wait—we put them in camps during WWII), the Asians, the Irish, the Germans, the Italians, the Jewish, the Indians, and many other ethnic groups from all over the world. Today we are reacting negatively and slowly to Hispanic and Muslim immigrants.

Yes, we are the "Land of Opportunity" and the country of "Bring us your Tired and Poor," but we cannot look at a nineteenth-century vision through a twenty-first century lens to make decisions concerning immigration. We must develop a vision of who we are concerning immigration in the twenty-first century. That cannot and should not be developed through politically motivated contact lenses. Again, we have all the stakeholders we need to develop a vision for who the United States of American should be in the twenty-first century. Until that happens, we will continue to pass laws and make decisions based on political ideology rather than who we need to be as a united country.

We have been that "shining beacon" to the world because we are the world (see above) and it is our responsibility to remain that beacon. The world depends on that. We can have secure borders and still have an immigration system that accepts the "Tired and Poor" and protects the "Land of Opportunity" through a twenty-first-century immigration vision. This will not happen if greed and selfishness continue to dominate the rhetoric and decision-making.

GUN RIGHTS OR GUN CONTROL: TO HAVE GUNS OR TO NOT HAVE GUNS—IS THAT THE QUESTION?

I feel like this is the third verse of the same song. Communication, distorted by political ideology, has created so many factually untrue statements that the American people are divided into political camps and no one is asking the real questions that need to be asked before having a safe and secure nation is possible. Our challenge in dealing with the question to have guns or to not have guns may or may not be the complete question or issue. We must stop the rhetoric that is causing nothing but divisiveness and begin gathering and discussing factual positive information that will guide us to the conclusion of how to make our schools, workplaces, theaters, restaurants, concert venues, churches, etc. safe and secure again. Do we have the stakeholders with motivation to solve this issue? Why aren't we utilizing them in solving the issues concerning the safety of our country?

The Second Amendment is there for a reason. That eighteenth-century reason, as with immigration, must be clarified through a twenty-first-century lens. What we are doing now as American citizens, lobbyists, and political leaders is a disgrace to the United States of America. We appear to be having an arms race among ourselves while American men, women, and children are dying. We can do better than having "warning signs" in our schools to remind our five- to seventeen-year-old students every day when they come to school of the fear that exists in our schools today. Greed and selfishness are in complete control of this issue.

YES, THE CLIMATE IS CHANGING!

A LITTLE DIFFERENT SONG which we sing to the same tune. Communication, distorted by political ideology, has created so many factually untrue statements concerning climate change that the American people are divided into political camps. The difference with this song is that we have been asking the real questions for years and have so much information that our challenge is to take the information and independently validate what we need to do.

The climate is changing. Where I grew up, people would say, "If you don't like the weather, don't worry. It will change tomorrow." The problem has not been that climate changes. It always has. The problem is the changes are becoming more extreme. Parts of our nation have been through three "one-hundred-year floods" in the past seven to ten years. There seems to be agreement that the climate is changing. The disagreements seem to center on what is causing the severe climate change.

This issue carries with it an enormous economic ingredient that will affect negatively parts of our free market system. The last time we had such a major divisive issue, other than the depression in the 1930s and WWII in the 1940s, with the potential to negatively affect the nation's economy and change lifestyles as much as the climate change issue was in 1860. We did not handle that one very well either. This negative impact has and will devastate many American businesses and citizens. This must be at the forefront of any discussions concerning what we do.

We have a history as a nation of taking something away from businesses and citizens without replacing it with something that will help those affected. (I reference you to our history concerning civil rights as well as our current healthcare and immigration crisis.) We must involve those affected stakeholders in the discussion of the problem and potential solutions. We must work very closely with those parts of our free market system that will be most affected.

Many of these companies and organizations have done very well for themselves with greed and selfishness. They have been very divisive concerning the issue of climate change. Their rhetoric has been quick to belittle climate change but nonexistent in recommending what to do concerning the environmental disasters and global implications. There are too many unknown risks involved with the issue of climate change to ignore the potential disasters we have experienced and to ignore the question of what to do to protect our nation and planet.

The other major issue is the American people's standard of living. Many of the companies and organizations who would be most affected by some of the recommended changes provide products and services to the American people. These products and services have become the standard of living Americans are accustom to. Are the American people ready to adjust to a different, not less, style of living? Or are greed and selfishness more important than national security and safety concerning the environment? If you believe that greed and selfishness are not the issue, we need your input on what we need to do to protect our nation from the environment rather than rhetoric that does not include what your suggestions are for combating the devastation we are experiencing.

We have individuals on both sides of the climate change issue with the knowledge to solve this problem. It can be resolved by adding consensus and compromise to the greed and selfishness rhetoric that has dominated this issue.

WHERE DO WE WANT THE UNITED STATES OF AMERICA TO GO?

Some might think that the best way to get consensus and compromise in our government is to—using two titles that many people in the United States would consider oxymoronic statements—elect liberal Republicans and conservative Democrats. This would probably get consensus and compromise but at the expense of losing the positive impact and contribution of conservative Republicans and liberal Democrats and most independents. Most importantly, we would be losing a large and influential part of our nation who have the beliefs and values of those who were pioneers that helped build this wonderful country of ours. We would be out of balance concerning consensus, compromise, greed, and selfishness. We would not consistently make the right decisions, and I also believe our country would be more divisive than we are now.

We must solve these issues without severely dividing our country. It is going to take a balance among consensus, compromise, greed, and selfishness to solve these issues because the dominate imbalance of greed and selfishness is destroying our country. Greed and selfishness can destroy many ethical values, but the value it affects most is trust. Individuals, groups, businesses, governments, or nations that function out of greed and selfishness become known as not worthy of trust. When trust is lost, it is not something that is easy or quick to regain.

We as individuals and as a nation must start listening with respect rather than ignoring someone we don't agree with. We must communicate and act as respectful, secure "winners" rather than disrespectful, insecure "losers." We must regain our vision and value for free speech. We must stop manipulating and gerrymandering our structure of governing. We must stop using religion to divide our nation and bridge the gap between freedom for religion and freedom from religion. We must identify and correct the distorted political ideology communications that create factually untrue statements. And we must reacquaint ourselves with what a true democracy means.

The issue of whether we can balance consensus, compromise, greed, and selfishness will not be decided by politicians. It will be decided by the American people. People do what they get rewarded for doing. If we continue rewarding our elected officials with reelection for dividing the country and bringing our government to gridlock, or if we continue rewarding disrespectful, insecure "losers" for their negative communications, bending or breaking the rules, or manipulating situations, then we, the American people, are to be blamed and held responsible for the effects of the gridlock and divisiveness in our nation's future.

What we, the American people, need from our elected officials/government are plans on how to solve the major issues in our country. What our elected officials/government need is a factually based, impartial process of making decisions. They need help and guidance from the American people.

The American people and our elected representatives need decision-making processes that will add clarity to the, sometimes dysfunctional, dialogue that exists concerning our more divisive issues. We need impartial individuals and/or groups with expertise in building compromise and consensus. These individuals can create and coordinate groups of stakeholders and congressional representatives with input from governmental related individuals. Their purpose will be to research and develop recommendations concerning the most divisive and controversial issues facing our country. The information and recommendations would be made available to the three branches of government and the American people. This would provide a degree of clarity to our government and the American people and provide a factual source of information for making their decisions concerning the future of our country. This process will also balance the relationship among consensus, compromise, greed, and selfishness, it will provide the structures and processes necessary for rebuilding trust, and it will prevent the possibility of preconceived solution syndrome.

I know there are people, organizations, and businesses that do not want to compromise or have consensus. They are doing very well with greed and selfishness. They do not have the motivation to change the direction that the state of our union is going in. We must help them understand that our country needs them and their contributions as well to be successful as "United" states and territories.

I am not advocating changing people's values and beliefs or their desires and rights. Those values, beliefs, desires, and rights are at the heart of who we are as Americans. I am not advocating changing our governing structure or changing that our elected and appointed officials make the decisions that govern our nation. That is the structure that is the envy of the world when it runs properly as designed. I am not advocating that voters should change who they voted for and elect different people. Our freedom to vote for who we want is the strength of this great nation. The people we elect give us equal representation, our advocates for freedom.

Last, but not least, is our process for the change of power in this country. The change of power process is the most valued part of our system that must be protected and continue to exist because it shows the world who we truly are as Americans.

CONCLUSION

IN MY WRITING CONCERNING communications, I described a nation so absorbed with their own ideologies that they do not respect those with a different ideology. I also described a nation whose basic communication responses and actions mirror those of a disrespectful insecure "loser's" responses and actions. In my writing concerning free speech, I described a nation that may be losing the vision and value for freedom of speech. In my writing concerning abortion, I described a nation so consumed with the issue of legality that it has ignored the real issues. In my writing concerning religion, I described a nation, created on freedom of religion, divided between freedom for religion and freedom from religion because of the blurring between politics and religion. In my writing concerning healthcare, I described a nation, founded on democratic free market principles, considering the government operate and coordinate their healthcare system because the American citizens, our free market economic system, and our political ideologies have not allowed us to solve the healthcare crisis and have created gridlock decision-making. In my writing concerning immigration, I described a process being taken by our national leaders to undermine the Constitution with an authoritative dictatorial leadership style and a nation in political denial concerning these actions and issues. I also described a nation that has lost sight of our immigration values and seems unwilling to develop a twenty-first-century vision of values to restore our leadership status in the world. In my writing concerning the integrity of the Constitution and the Supreme Court, I described a nation willing to severely tarnish the credibility of one of the three branches of our governing structure by gerrymandering rules and ethics to affect the selection process of justices. In my writing concerning a safe and secure nation, I described a nation that is completely controlled by greed and selfishness. In my writing concerning climate change, I described a nation unwilling to address the potential devasting environmental and economic risks because of economic greed and selfishness. In my writing concerning the role and size of government, I described a nation that cannot solve its own problems and issues, so the government solves them. I also described a nation that is both the cause and solution to the role and size of government but will not accept the responsibility to be a true democracy.

This does not sound like a democracy. It sounds more like turmoil that could lead to the beginning of a dictatorship, religious state, socialism, or communism. Any other form of government, except democracy, is not acceptable and would be devastating. When you stop laughing about this statement, you will be where I was when I heard that the United States of America will not exist in one hundred years. Could this really happen?

The state of our union is under attack. We have adversaries in the world that do not want to go to war with our military, but they can and are at war with the people of the United States of America by undermining our democratic form of government through their divisive methods. We must not allow this strategy of divide and conquer to succeed.

A true democracy is never easy, always emotional, usually looks out of control, wins and loses but never gives up and continually seeks to be united. You may think that having a true democracy is a pipe dream, but this dream pales in comparison to the pipe dream of 1776.

There is a TV series entitled *This Is Us* that many Americans are watching. It is a story about a diverse family's journey through life together. It contains the successes and the failures, the happiness and the tragedies, the agreements and the arguments, and the union and the divisiveness. The family struggles to remain united. Each week the TV series brings a new issue to deal with.

"We the People" are also *This Is Us,* and we must continue to struggle to remain united. To think we cannot remain united is ludicrous. We are the United States of America. *Yes, we can make America great again.*

The changes we need to make, to use another old saying, "Are not a destination. They are a journey." A journey we have been on for over 225 years. This is us, America. We are the people who have everything we need to make the state of our union a success. We need to stop counting the issues that are divisive to us and start counting the blessings that this great nation has offered and will continue to offer to us if we will come together on one goal.

To be united!

ABOUT THE AUTHOR

During my career, I have been self-employed in a service-related business with twenty-six employees I hired and was responsible for and to. I also worked in finance and credit management for the largest retailer in the nation at that time.

Most of my career was spent in postsecondary education and training. During that time, I was affiliated with three different colleges. I taught management, accounting, marketing, and other business-related courses. I also consulted with and trained employees of business and industry located in the geographic areas of these three colleges. The topics and assignments included quality management and leadership, strategic planning, team building and decision-making, continuous process management and improvement, and organizational development and management.

I spent over ten years in human resources with an organization that employed over 20,000 individuals, of which over 15,000 were benefited employees. Most of my time was spent in the position of executive director of the compensation and benefits department. The department's responsibilities included developing and maintaining salary schedules and reclassification procedures, developing and maintaining benefits for all eligible employees and implementation of guidelines associated with immigration and naturalization.

ABOUT THE BOOK

THE MOTIVATION BEHIND THE writing of "Where Did the United States of America Go" is to offer a series of reflections on the current state of our union and the causes of the divisive issues plaguing our nation. The writing offers a nonpartisan insight into the government's and electorate's failings. The purpose of the writing is to offer a measured approach, refraining from hasty judgements that would alienate the reader rather than help the reader better understand, cope with, and involve themselves in the changes that are affecting our democracy.

www.ingramcontent.com/pod-product-compliance
Lightning Source LLC
Chambersburg PA
CBHW051413250726

48655CB00003B/1028